W9-BQS-370

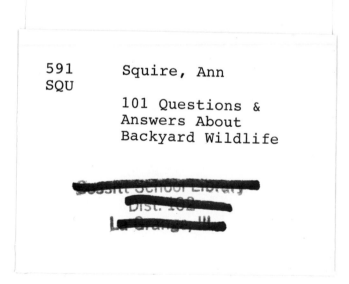

591
SQU

Squire, Ann

101 Questions &
Answers About
Backyard Wildlife

101

Questions & Answers

About

Backyard Wildlife

Ann Squire

Illustrations by Jennifer DiRubbio

Walker and Company
New York

101 Questions & Answers About Backyard Wildlife

First published in the United States of America in 1996 by Walker Publishing Company, Inc.

Published simultaneously in Canada by Thomas Allen & Son Canada, Limited, Markham, Ontario

Library of Congress Cataloging-in-Publication Data
Squire, Ann.
101 questions & answers about backyard wildlife / Ann Squire: illustrations by Jennifer DiRubbio.
p.   cm.
Summary: Uses a question-and-answer format to present information about various birds, insects, mammals, and reptiles.
Includes index.
ISBN 0-8027-8457-7 (hardcover).
—ISBN 0-8027-8458-5 (reinforced)
1. Animals—Miscellanea—Juvenile literature.
[1. Animals—Miscellanea.   2. Questions and answers.]
I. DiRubbio, Jennifer, ill.   II. Title.
QL49.S672   1996
591—dc20   96-25408
                                                      CIP
                                                       AC

BOOK DESIGN BY CAROL MALCOLM RUSSO/SIGNET M DESIGN, INC.

Printed in the United States of America
10 9 8 7 6 5 4 3 2 1

Contents

Author's Note

The inspiration to write *101 Questions & Answers About Backyard Wildlife* arose when my family and I bought a large, old house a few years ago. After moving in, I was astonished by the incredible variety of wild animals—ants, termites, wasps, squirrels, and more—to be found in and around a dwelling designed for people.

As an animal behaviorist, I've studied my share of exotic wildlife, including African electric fish and creatures of the coral reef. I soon realized, however, that I knew next to nothing about the birds, bugs, and other beasts living around (and often in) my own home.

My research into the habits and behaviors of backyard wildlife has shown me that even the most ordinary creatures can be as strange and fascinating as anything one might encounter on safari or in the zoo. I hope my readers will feel the same way after delving into the secret lives of the animals in their backyards.

101
Questions & Answers
About
Backyard Wildlife

1

Feathers, Feet, & Other Bird Facts

1. When I'm in the park, I sometimes see pigeons turning around in circles and chasing each other. What are they doing?

If you spend an hour or so at a city park, especially during the spring and summer, you'll see many different pigeon behaviors. One of the most fascinating is the bowing display, usually performed by the male. When he wants to impress a female, the male pigeon runs after her with his head held high, his tail feathers fanned out, and the feathers on his neck and back puffed up. (To anyone watching, it seems that he wants to appear as large and important as possible.) When he reaches the female, the male bows his head, coos loudly and turns in a circle, sweeping his spread tail feathers against the ground.

Pigeons also perform the bowing display when approached by birds they do not know. Their goal in this case is also to look imposing, but for a very different reason: to frighten away the intruder.

How do you know if a bowing pigeon is showing off to a potential mate or threatening a stranger? One small difference makes it easy to tell these two displays apart. A pigeon displaying to a female spreads his tail feathers wide. If he is bowing to a stranger, he keeps his tail feathers folded.

2. Where do city pigeons build their nests?

Pigeons are a common sight in many U.S. cities, yet most people have never seen a pigeon's nest. Why not? Urban pigeons are secretive nesters. They roost in sheltered, out-of-the-way places such as air vents, crevices in buildings, and window ledges high above the street. These habits are not too surprising, since the wild relative of these birds, the European rock dove, builds its nests on rocky ledges, and in caves and holes in cliffs. The high-rise buildings in most cities provide an excellent substitute, making pigeons feel right at home in urban areas.

To spot a city pigeon's nest, which usually consists of little more than some sticks or pieces of straw, be on the lookout for dark, sheltered spots high off the ground. The girders and beams underneath bridges are particularly good places to look.

3. How do owls hunt so well in the dark?

Because owls hunt at night, they depend on keen vision and hearing to locate mice and rats scurrying through the underbrush. While their vision is excellent, the hearing of some owls is truly amazing. The barn owl, for example, can hunt in total darkness, using only its sense of hearing to find and home in on its prey.

How does the barn owl do it? For one thing, it has big ears. In fact, the owl's eardrums are larger than those of any other bird. The barn owl also has movable ear flaps that can be pointed in the direction of a sound, and short feathers around the ear that work like miniature satellite dishes to channel sounds into the ear opening. And strangest of all, one ear is located higher up on the head than the other ear!

This unusual arrangement makes it possible for the barn owl to pinpoint the exact location of a sound, even in complete darkness. Specifically, the bird pays attention to the small interval between the times when sounds arrive at the left and right ears.

Imagine an owl perched on a tree limb, listening carefully for the sound of a mouse scampering along the ground. If the mouse is on the owl's right, the sound will reach the bird's right ear slightly before it reaches the left ear. Immediately, the owl turns its head to the right, until the sound strikes both ears at the same time. Now the owl is facing in the direction of its prey.

Next the owl must decide whether the sound comes from above or below. Because of its uneven ears, sounds from below will reach the left ear first. The owl then lowers its head until the sound is equal in the left and right ears. When this happens, the bird is facing the mouse, even though neither can see the other.

Although it sounds very complicated, this whole process, from first hearing the mouse to leaving the perch, takes the owl less than half a second!

4. How do owls hunt so silently?

Because they hunt in the dark of night, owls rely on their keen sense of hearing to detect the faint rustling of mice and other small prey. But these animals have excellent hearing, too, and survive by being very alert to danger. To avoid scaring away a potential meal, owls must make as little noise as possible while hunting.

Owls have two important attributes that help them sneak up on their prey. First, they are able to fly in almost complete silence, thanks to the soft edges on their flight feathers. Second, owls have very large wings in relation to their body weight. This makes flying almost effortless and eliminates the need for a lot of wing flapping. In fact, an owl's final approach to its victim is usually a swift, silent, and deadly glide.

5. What are owl pellets?

One clue that there are owls in your neighborhood is the presence of small, hard pellets that you may find on the ground under trees or in barns or abandoned buildings where owls have made their nests.

Because owls swallow their food whole, they end up eating things they cannot digest, such as bones and fur (if the prey was a rodent) or feathers (if it was a small bird). A few hours to a day after eating, the owl regurgitates a compact pellet made up of these undigested parts.

If you do find an owl pellet, look at it closely, and

you may be able to tell what kind of animal was un-lucky enough to be the owl's last meal.

6. How can I make an easy nesting box for birds?

Providing a sheltered spot for birds to nest and raise their young is a great way to attract them to your yard. While some bird species require specially con-structed nest boxes, wrens will happily use a simple house made from a gourd that you can grow in your own garden.

Here's how to create your own gourd birdhouse:

1. At your hardware store or garden center, buy a package of ornamental gourd seeds, then plant them outdoors in early spring. Watch the climbing vine with its pear-shaped gourds grow throughout the summer.

2. In the fall, harvest your gourds when their color changes from green to tan. Be sure to leave a few inches of stem attached. Place the gourds in a warm, well-ventilated place for several months to dry.

3. When the seeds rattle inside, your gourd is dry. Wash it well, and waterproof it by painting it with

two coats of polyurethane. Use a sharp knife to cut a one-and-one-half-inch hole four to six inches up from the bottom of the gourd. Poke a long stick or spoon handle into the hole to loosen the fibers and seeds, and shake them out.

4. Attach wire to the stem, and hang the gourd from a tree branch six to ten feet above the ground.

5. Watch and wait for your new tenants to move in!

7. How can I attract woodpeckers to my yard?

If you are a beginning bird-watcher, you may have trouble identifying some of the species that flit through your backyard. But the rat-tat-tat of a woodpecker drumming on a tree trunk is an unmistakable sign that one of these fascinating birds is in the neighborhood. To attract more, make your own woodpecker feeding station.

Woodpeckers eat mostly insects and grubs, which they find by pecking into small crevices and holes in the bark of trees. To make a woodpecker feeder, use a screwdriver to bore several deep holes in a piece of rotten log. Then stuff the holes with suet mixed with bird seed. (You can buy suet and seed cakes at the hardware store or supermarket.) Finally, hang the feeder from a tree branch, and wait for some woodpeckers to show up for dinner.

8. What backyard animal has the most amazing tongue?

One of the most incredible tongues in the animal world belongs to the woodpecker. Whereas humans use their tongues to taste food, the woodpecker uses its tongue as a hunting weapon to capture its prey. After boring into a tree trunk with its powerful bill, the woodpecker inserts its long tongue deep into the hole it has made, where it probes for insects. Many woodpeckers have sticky tongues or tiny hooks and barbs on the tongue tip. Both of these features help the bird extract as many insects as possible from beneath the tree bark.

Perhaps the most amazing thing about a woodpecker's tongue is its length: Some woodpeckers can extend their tongues six inches beyond the tip of their bills!

9. Why don't birds sing in the winter?

One reason you don't hear birds singing in the colder months is that many species are gone, having migrated south for the winter. But some birds, such as starlings, mourning doves, and sparrows, are around all winter. Yet even they are silent.

For birds, singing is associated with mating. As birds mate and begin to build their nests, one of their first tasks is to stake out a territory where other birds are not welcome. By keeping competitors away from a particular area, a nesting bird ensures that there will be enough food for both parents and the growing chicks. Singing is a very effective way of announcing to other birds, "This territory is occupied!"

Since most birds set up territories and mate in the spring, this is the time you are most likely to hear birdsong.

10. Why do migrating ducks and geese fly in a V formation?

Nearly everyone has spotted the familiar V shape of a group of geese or ducks flying overhead. Yet scientists aren't really sure why this behavior occurs. Some believe that each bird in the V receives lift from the bird in front of it. (Lift, an upward draft created by air currents rushing over and under the wing, is also what gets airplanes off the ground.) By staying in close V formation, each bird, except the leader, may get enough of a lift that it can fly longer with less effort.

It may also be that the V formation helps birds

avoid midair collisions, because each bird knows its position and can see the other members of the flock.

11. What are those little brown birds that are so common in city parks?

Next to the pigeon, the house sparrow is probably the bird seen most often in U.S. cities. House sparrows live in all fifty states, and in parts of Canada and Mexico as well. Surprisingly, these birds are not native to the United States and have been here only since the 1800s.

The first house sparrows to come to the United States lived in Brooklyn, New York, where eight pairs were released in 1850. All these birds died, however, and in 1852, another fifty birds were set free in Brooklyn's Greenwood Cemetery. This time the sparrows not only survived but within ten years had moved as far north as Maine and as far south as North Carolina. By 1900, the house sparrow was the most common bird in U.S. cities. Today there are so many of these little brown birds that people often consider them to be pests.

12. What backyard bird has the most amazing powers of flight?

The most incredible bird you're likely to see in the backyard—or anywhere else—is a hummingbird. Unlike most birds, which can only fly in a forward direction, hummingbirds are equally comfortable flying forward, backward, upside down, or even hovering in one place like a helicopter.

The hummingbird's amazing flying ability is the result of a very flexible shoulder joint. This allows the bird's wings to move in all directions, rather than just up and down. When hovering, for example, a hummingbird moves its wings forward and backward in a figure-eight pattern at the rate of 3,000 or more wingbeats per minute!

Even when it wants to move a short distance

along a branch or change position in its nest, the hummingbird flies rather than walking or hopping. Some scientists believe that hummingbirds fly because they are unable to walk.

13. How can I attract hummingbirds to my yard?

Even more than most birds, hummingbirds must eat almost constantly in order to survive, so the best way to attract them to your backyard is to feed them. The hummingbird's main food is nectar from flowers, and each tiny bird must visit more than 1,000 flowers a day to get enough to eat.

The hummingbird's long, slender bill is specially shaped to probe deep into the center of a flower to reach the nectar. The flowers most often visited by hummingbirds are long, trumpet shaped,  and red. You'll have a good chance of spotting some hummingbirds if you plant flowers that they like. These include honeysuckle, hibiscus, flowering tobacco, cardinal flower, morning glory, and bee balm. You can buy most of these plants at your local garden center.

Even if you don't have a garden, you can still attract hummingbirds by putting up a hummingbird feeder filled with a solution of sugar and water. Many books on birds and bird feeding include instructions on setting up a hummingbird feeder.

14. Why do birds build nests?

Many people mistakenly think that birds live in their nests all the time, just as people live in houses. In reality, birds use nests only when they are sitting on eggs or caring for chicks. Whether the nest is a hole in a tree, a cup made of sticks, or a burrow in the ground, it has several advantages for birds raising their young.

❊ The nest insulates the eggs and helps keep them warm even when the temperature falls at night.

❊ Tree-hole nests shelter the developing eggs from high heat and bright sun during the day.

❊ Nests in holes or burrows hide the eggs from predators.

❊ The cup- or pouch-shaped nests of many tree-living birds prevent the eggs from rolling out of the tree and onto the ground.

Whatever type of nest they build, the birds only use it until their chicks have grown. Then the whole family flies the coop.

15. Are there any backyard birds that don't build nests?

In a world where most birds spend a lot of time and effort building nests and raising young, the cowbird is unique. This species, which lives in suburban backyards throughout North America, manages to reproduce each year without doing much work at all. Instead of building its own nest, the cowbird lays its eggs in the nests of other birds, who then raise the cowbird chick as their own.

At the beginning of the breeding season, the female cowbird scouts around for suitable nests. Song sparrows, warblers, and vireos all make good foster parents. When she sees that the nest owners are not at home, the cowbird sneaks in and lays her own egg, sometimes removing any eggs that are already in the nest.

If the cowbird is lucky, the returning birds will not notice the switch and will devote themselves to incubating the egg and caring for the fast-growing chick. The young cowbird often gets much larger than its foster parents, who must work around the clock to satisfy its voracious appetite.

Unfortunately for the cowbird, her trick usually doesn't work. The returning birds see the strange egg and promptly toss it out of the nest. To make up for these failures, the cowbird needs to lay a lot of eggs in many different nests. Of the forty eggs a cowbird lays during a typical breeding season, only one or two of them will result in a new generation of cowbirds.

16. Why do ducks preen their feathers?

Watch a group of ducks floating on a pond, and sooner or later you'll see the following behavior: One duck suddenly swivels its head around and nibbles at the base of its tail. Then, using its bill, the duck strokes and smooths the feathers all over its back, wings, and breast. Every so often it turns to gnaw at its tail and then begins grooming all over again.

The behavior you're watching is more than simple preening and scratching—the duck is actually waterproofing its body! It dips its beak into an oil gland at the base of the tail and then spreads the oil over its feathers.

Once the feathers are coated with a thin film of oil, water just rolls off, and the bird stays warm and dry even in the worst weather.

17. Do birds hibernate?

Many birds cope with winter's cold temperatures and lack of food by migrating to warmer climates. Others stay put and manage to find enough to eat

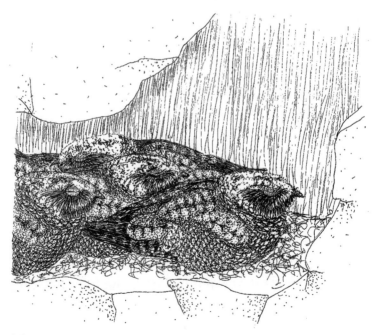

until spring comes. Only one North American bird, the poorwill, actually hibernates.

When the weather gets cold and food becomes scarce, poorwills huddle together in cliff crevices. Their body temperature drops to around 64 degrees (compared to a normal temperature of 106 degrees). Heartbeat and breathing slow down so much that the birds have been mistaken for dead. A hibernating poorwill can survive for three months without food or water before the warm days of spring tell the bird it's time to wake up.

18. How high do migrating birds fly?

Most people know that birds migrate, but many have never actually seen a migrating bird. One reason is that some migrants fly so high it's nearly impossible to spot them. Starlings and swallows fly fairly low— one-half to three-quarters of a mile in the air. The real champions are geese, ducks, and swans, which have been spotted on radar at altitudes of over two miles. These high-altitude migrants are often the fastest flyers, reaching speeds of eighty-five miles per hour.

19. Is there really a bird called a Baltimore oriole?

Yes. The Baltimore oriole is a bright orange bird with a jet-black head, just the same colors as the baseball team with the same name. The Baltimore oriole winters in the tropics and spends the spring and summer throughout the United States.

Look for the oriole's basketlike nest hanging from a tree branch up to sixty feet above the ground. Since orioles enjoy fruit nectar, you can encourage them to visit your yard by putting out cut oranges and grapefruits. Baltimore orioles will also drink sugar water from hummingbird feeders.

20. Why do some gulls have a bright red spot on the tip of the bill?

Next time you're at the beach or at a city pier, take a look at the gulls around you. Chances are, some of them will be sporting a bright red patch at the tip of the lower bill. For years, scientists had no idea what purpose the red spot could possibly serve. Finally, it

was discovered that baby gulls use the patch as a "target" when begging for food. When a gull chick pecks at the red spot on its parent's bill, the adult responds by giving the chick a bit of food.

The scientist who studied this behavior found that the red patch was all-important. If the spot was painted over, the chicks stopped pecking—and got nothing to eat!

21. What backyard birds have the best hearing?

A good sense of hearing is crucial for birds, especially for those that communicate through calls and songs and those that rely on sound to find food. The best sense of hearing may belong to the barn owl, which can capture mice in total darkness by listening to the faint sounds these rodents make as they move through the grass. Another bird with excellent hearing is the American robin. When you see a robin standing motionless on the lawn with its head cocked to one side, you can be pretty sure that it is straining to hear earthworms moving underground. Even the common pigeon has keen hearing, and scientists believe that pigeons can detect faint vibrations from movements in the earth's crust thousands of miles away.

22. How fast does a flying bird flap its wings?

The tiny hummingbird flaps its wings faster than any other bird—sometimes more than 3,000 wingbeats per minute. At this speed, the bird's wings appear as a blur, and scientists must use strobe lights and other special equipment to count the wingbeats.

The common gull is one of the slowest flappers, beating its wings fewer than three times a second while flying. Of course, gulls can also soar for long periods without flapping their wings at all, which is something a hummingbird could never do. Most

backyard birds fall somewhere in between the fre-
netic hummingbird and the casually soaring gull.

23. What can you learn by looking at a bird's feet?

Different birds have very different kinds of feet, and
looking at a bird's feet can tell you a lot about how,
and even where, the bird lives. Ducks, for instance,
have broad, webbed feet that work like oars to propel
them through the water. With feet like these, a duck
could never perch on a slender tree limb. For that job,
a bird needs feet like those of sparrows, finches, and
other perching birds. These birds have slender, flexible toes (three pointing forward and one pointing
backward) that wrap securely around even the
thinnest branches. Woodpeckers, which cling to tree
trunks as they drill for food, have two of their toes (instead of just one) pointing backward for extra support.

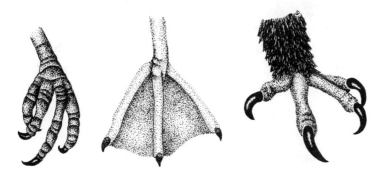

Birds of prey such as owls and eagles have powerful feet and razor-sharp curved claws so that they can grab and carry small animals. The osprey, which eats fish, even has spines on the pads of its feet to help it hold on to its slippery prey.

24. What determines the shape of an egg?

Think of an egg, and you'll probably visualize a typical chicken egg: rounded on one end and slightly pointed on the other. In fact, the eggs of different birds come in different shapes, from almost perfectly round to very long and pointed on one or both ends.

The shape of a bird's egg has a lot to do with where it is laid. Many shorebirds that make their nests on narrow rock ledges lay eggs that are round on one end and sharply pointed on the other. If accidentally pushed, the egg will roll around in a circle rather than rolling straight off the edge of the cliff.

Birds such as robins and bluebirds build cup-shaped nests that offer a bit more protection than exposed ledges. These birds lay eggs that are a little rounder than the pointed eggs of shorebirds.

The roundest eggs of all are laid by birds that nest in tree holes or underground burrows. Since there is almost no danger of the eggs rolling out of the nest, there is no need for them to be very pointed at one end. Birds that lay round eggs include burrowing owls, which nest in underground holes, and woodpeckers, which nest in holes in tree trunks.

25. Why don't birds have teeth?

Because they weigh too much! In order to get off the ground—and stay aloft—birds need to be as lightweight as possible. And as airplane designers know, a flying machine is easiest to control if most of the weight is concentrated in the center. So a mouthful of heavy teeth at the front end is a luxury birds cannot afford.

Instead of teeth, birds have beaks. Beaks vary quite a bit in size and shape, but they all have one thing in common: They don't weigh very much. Even the toucan's oversized bill is much lighter than it looks.

One drawback to a bill is that a bird can't chew up its food. To solve that problem, birds have gizzards. After the bird gulps its food down whole, this muscular pouch grinds it up. Birds sometimes swallow small pieces of sand or gravel to help the gizzard do its grinding work. Although the gravel adds some weight, it is located right in the center of the bird— just where the airplane designers say it should be.

26. How does a woodpecker peck without giving itself a headache?

Woodpeckers peck for several reasons: to signal to other birds, to probe for food, or to excavate a nest hole. During the breeding season, a male woodpecker can spend up to five hours at a stretch chipping out a nest hole in a tree. With all that pecking, you'd expect a woodpecker to end each day with a splitting headache or even a concussion.

There are two reasons this doesn't happen. First of all, between the bird's upper bill and skull, there is a soft and spongy cushion of cartilage. This cartilage acts as a natural shock absorber, softening the impact of the bird's forceful pecks.

Second, the woodpecker's brain is doubly protected: Not only is it encased in a muscular, shock-absorbing sling, but it fits so snugly inside the head that it doesn't bounce around and get damaged as the woodpecker pecks.

27. How can birds balance on one leg without falling over?

If you have ever tried to stand on one foot for more than a few minutes, you probably found it extremely difficult to maintain your balance. Yet most birds, from a tiny sparrow perching on a tree to a gangly flamingo at the zoo, seem to perform this balancing act with ease.

One difference between a bird and a person is that the bird's legs are usually quite slender, accounting for only a fraction of its total weight. This means that the bird can pull one leg up without shifting its body weight too much. Human legs are, proportionally, much heavier, so lifting up one leg alters dramatically a person's center of gravity and makes it much harder to balance.

In addition, most birds have big feet with wide-spread toes, which serve as a large "platform" on which to balance. Perching birds such as sparrows have another advantage: They possess powerful toes that they can wrap tightly around a branch, anchoring them to one spot. Some birds are so good at balancing on one leg that they can do this even in high winds and stormy weather.

28. Do birds' feathers ever wear out?

Even though most birds spend lots of time preening and grooming, feathers eventually become tattered and worn. When this happens, they must be replaced. Feathers are usually replaced once a year in a process called molting, when the old feathers fall

out or are pushed out by new ones growing underneath.

Because a bird needs to be able to fly to escape danger and find food, it cannot afford to lose all its feathers at once. For this reason, molting is a gradual process, with just a few feathers being lost at a time. The change is so subtle that you've probably seen backyard birds in the process of molting and never even noticed it.

Birds that live on ponds or in marshlands can often find food without flying, and some of them, including ducks and cranes, lose all their flight feathers at once.

Only one bird, the penguin, goes on a starvation diet while it molts. Most penguins live on fish, which they catch while "flying" underwater. Without a completely waterproof covering of feathers, penguins would quickly freeze in the icy water. During the several weeks it takes them to molt, the ragged-looking penguins remain on land, eating nothing, as their tiny feathers fall out in clumps, only to be replaced by a shiny new waterproof suit of armor.

2

Bees, Butterflies, & Other Bugs

29. Why do fireflies flash?

The greenish yellow glow of fireflies is a common sight in the suburbs and country-side on early-summer evenings. The best time to spot them is around dusk in an area with low shrubs and open lawns. Fireflies use their lights to signal to each other, but the signals are for one purpose only—find-ing a mate—and the only time that fireflies flash is during their brief mating season in early summer.

The fireflies you're most likely to see are the males, as they cruise slowly around your yard about two feet above the ground, flashing their lights on and off. These roving males are "advertising" to female fireflies, who sit motionless on the leaves of shrubs or plants, waiting for the right male to come along. When she recognizes a male of her species (from the color, length, or timing of his flash), the female flashes in response. The time between his flash and her answering flash is very important. If she responds too soon or not

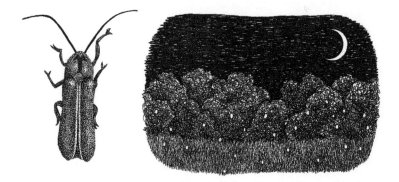

soon enough, the male will pass her by. But if the timing of her answering flash is just right, the male knows that he has found a female of his own species, and he flies over to join her.

Unfortunately for some male fireflies, this system can backfire. Female fireflies of the genus *Photuris* have the ability to impersonate other females, including those from the genus *Photinus*. When a hungry *Photuris* female spots a flashing *Photinus* male, she imitates the flash pattern of a

Photinus female. Fooled by her signal, the unsuspecting male flies over to meet her and is devoured.

30. What are some other amazing facts about fireflies?

❀ One species of firefly, *Pyrophorus noctilucus,* produces a glow so bright that South American natives once used it for light by trapping several of these fireflies inside a lantern. It would take 150 of our North American fireflies to equal the light of one *Pyrophorus.*

❀ Fireflies generate lots of light but not much heat. Their "cold" light is much more efficient than that of an electric light bulb, which gives off a great deal of warmth along with its light.

31. How can I stop yellow jackets from buzzing around the food at my picnic?

If you have ever had a summer picnic, you've probably been annoyed by these black-and-yellow-striped scavengers. While it is difficult to get rid of them once they have decided to share your lunch, the best way to avoid yellow jackets in the first place is to have your outdoor picnics early in the summer.

Hornets and yellow jackets don't become active until late spring, when the queens come out of the protected crevices where they have spent the winter. They get right to work building their papery nests. After constructing just a few six-sided cells, the queen lays an egg in each one. In a few weeks, full-grown female workers emerge and begin their job of helping the queen enlarge the nest and tend to developing young.

There are two reasons that early-summer yellow jackets don't bother people. The first is that, at the beginning of summer, there are very few of these insects, but by summer's end, the colony has grown to include hundreds of individuals. And second, the early-season yellow jackets are simply too busy building the nest, finding food, and caring for young to come to a picnic.

By late summer, however, the yellow jackets' society begins to fall apart. The queen stops laying eggs, and soon there is nothing for the workers to do. They spend less and less time at the hive and begin to forage on their own for food. Because they like fruits and sweet liquids, it is easy to spot them around trash cans or anywhere that people have discarded soft drink containers or food wrappers. It is this late-summer scavenging behavior that brings these insects to your picnic, and it's the reason that yellow jackets are a bigger problem on Labor Day than they were on Memorial Day.

32. How do houseflies walk on the ceiling?

Flies are well known for their amazing ability to walk on walls, windows, and even ceilings without falling off. How do they do it?

These insects have highly specialized feet that help them resist the pull of gravity no matter where they are standing. On rough surfaces, such as textured ceilings, the fly uses claws at the tip of each foot to grasp and hold on to tiny bumps and projections. To walk on glass and other smooth surfaces, the fly literally glues itself to the spot, using a sticky substance produced by pads on each foot.

33. What happens to butterflies in the winter?

The various butterflies you may see in your garden during the summer have a number of ways of coping with—or escaping—the winter cold. Many butterflies spend the winter in a dormant state, where they remain still and neither eat nor move around. Some butterflies lay eggs that do not hatch until spring, while others spend the winter as caterpillars.

But the most amazing winter strategy is that of the monarch butterfly, which travels south as far as 2,000 miles from its habitats in northeastern, midwestern, and parts of western North America to wintering spots in Mexico and southern California. Flying at an average speed of twelve miles an hour, the monarch would have to fly nonstop for a week to complete its journey! (It does stop along the way, of course, to rest and eat, so the trip takes quite a bit longer.)

Adults that survive the storms and other dangers they encounter on the long trip will begin to fly north again in the spring, but not all of them will make it. After mating, the monarchs lay their eggs during their northward migration. Once they complete this important task, many of the butterflies die, leaving their offspring to finish the journey.

34. *Where can I see monarch butterflies?*

Monarch butterflies live in almost every part of North America except the Pacific Northwest. These orange-and-black butterflies are easiest to spot in fields, along roadsides, in weedy lots, or wherever the milkweed plant grows. Monarch butterflies lay their eggs only on milkweed, and this plant's leaves serve as food for developing caterpillars. So where you find milkweed, you will usually find monarchs.

If you are lucky enough to be in southern California in the fall and winter, it is worth a trip to the Monterey Peninsula to see the great swarms of monarch butterflies that roost in pine and eucalyptus trees in the small town of Pacific Grove. At night, the

butterflies cluster in the trees with their wings folded, looking like dead leaves. Then, warmed by the morning sun, hundreds of monarchs leave their roosts and flutter through the forest.

The butterflies begin to arrive in Pacific Grove every October and remain there for the winter. On the second Saturday of October, the schoolchildren of Pacific Grove dress in butterfly costumes and have a parade to celebrate the return of the migrating monarchs.

35. Why and how do bees make honey?

Bees don't make honey for people; they make it for themselves. Honey is one of the two foods that honeybees need for survival (the other is pollen), and a colony of 60,000 to 80,000 bees can eat nearly 200 pounds of honey a year.

The honey-making process starts at a flower, where a foraging bee collects a sugary liquid called nectar. When her stomach is full of nectar, the forager bee returns to the hive, where she transfers the nectar to a "house bee." (House bees get their name because they stay inside the hive feeding the young, cleaning up, and making honey.) After receiving the nectar from the forager, the house bee sits quietly, repeatedly opening and closing her mouthparts. As the nectar is exposed to the air, it becomes thicker and more concentrated. After about twenty minutes of "chewing," the bee puts the nectar into an empty cell in the honeycomb. Over the next few days, other bees fan the nectar with their wings, and it gradually turns into the thick, sweet substance we call honey.

36. How do butterflies, bees, and other insects know which flowers contain nectar?

Scent almost certainly plays a role in attracting insects to nectar-rich flowers. In addition, signals on the flower itself, such as stripes, spots, or patches of color, tell insects which flowers contain nectar and even point the way toward the flower's center, where the nectar is located. Foxgloves have tall spikes of tube-shaped flowers. Just inside each flower is a pattern of bright dots that may guide the bee deep inside the flower to the hidden nectar. The petals of some geraniums have lines that radiate from the flower's center, like the spokes of a wheel. Pansies sometimes also have these spokelike lines, and both pansies and primroses have a brightly colored patch at each flower's center.

Many other flowers have these special signals, called nectar guides. Some flowers even have nectar guides that are invisible to humans. However, bees and butterflies, which can detect ultraviolet light, can see them quite clearly.

37. What is unusual about a butterfly's feet?

Incredible as it may seem, butterflies can taste things with their feet, just as people taste with their tongues. This odd ability is actually very practical for the butterfly. Nectar-rich flowers often have sweet substances on their petals as well, so the butterfly can tell as soon as it lands on a blossom whether there is nectar inside.

Scientists have discovered that the taste organs in the feet of monarch butterflies are 2,500 times more sensitive than human taste buds.

38. Help! I've been stung! How can I tell if it was by a wasp or a bee?

Both wasps and bees have the ability to sting people, but they are far less likely to attack than most people imagine. If you have been stung, it is probably because you disturbed or threatened the insect.

The easiest way to tell if a wasp or a bee caused the sting is to look at the perpetrator. Both yellow jackets (the type of wasp you're most likely to see) and honeybees have yellow-and-black markings, and they look very much alike, but honeybees have hairy bodies, whereas the bodies of yellow jackets are smooth.

If the insect that stung you has flown away, you can sometimes identify the culprit by looking at the sting. Wasp stingers are smooth, rather like a needle. After piercing your skin and injecting its venom, the wasp slides its stinger out and flies away. Honeybees have barbed stingers (somewhat like fishhooks) that snag your skin and remain even after the bee has gone. When the bee leaves behind its stinger, it also leaves its venom sac. The muscles in this sac can continue pumping venom into the wound for up to twenty minutes.

39. Do all bees sting?

Only the females of bees, wasps, and hornets have the ability to sting. The stinger is a modified egg-laying tube (called an ovipositor). Since males do not lay eggs, they do not have ovipositors, so they are also unable to sting.

40. What do mosquitoes eat?

If you answered "blood," you're half right. Only female mosquitoes suck blood, and the main reason they do it isn't to get something to eat. In order for her eggs to develop, the female mosquito needs a meal of blood—and the bigger her meal, the more eggs she will produce.

After drinking your blood, the mosquito stops searching for victims. Instead she rests and after a time lays between 100 and 500 eggs. The whole cy-

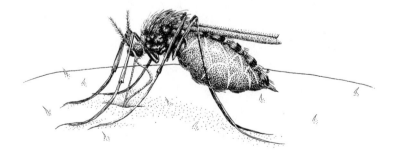

cle (from sucking your blood to laying her eggs) can take several days. Only after the eggs have been laid does the female mosquito start looking for another meal of blood.

Because male mosquitoes do not lay eggs, they have no need for blood. In fact, they do not even have the special mouthparts necessary to pierce skin. Both male and female mosquitoes get most of their nourishment by sipping the nectar from flowers.

41. Do all mosquitoes attack people?

Entomologists (scientists who study insects) estimate that there are 100 different mosquito species in North America, and nearly 3,000 species worldwide! Fortunately, not all of them prey on people. Some mosquitoes are not choosy and will drink blood from almost any animal that comes along. One example is an African mosquito that has been seen feeding on chickens, frogs, toads, monkeys, cattle, dogs, horses, donkeys, and elephants—in addition to humans! Other species are specialists, such as the tropical mosquito that preys only on ants.

42. How do caterpillars avoid being eaten by birds?

A caterpillar must eat almost constantly to store up the energy it needs to transform itself into an adult moth or butterfly. But a caterpillar sitting on a leaf can't crawl away quickly, which makes it an easy target for hungry birds. Caterpillars have developed some unusual ways to avoid being eaten while they're munching on leaves. Some have spiky hairs and spines, which get stuck in the throat of any animal foolish enough to try to eat

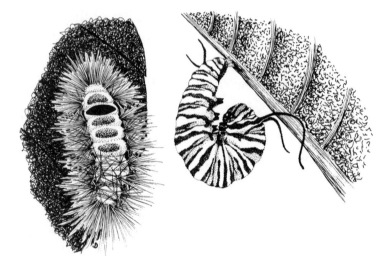

them. Others, such as monarch butterfly caterpillars, are poisonous, and it takes only one taste to teach a bird to leave them alone. Caterpillars that use these types of defenses usually have bright colors to warn away animals that might attack them.

Some caterpillars go to the other extreme and

avoid predators by hiding. The stick caterpillar feeds at night, when birds are not hunting for food. By day, this thin, brown caterpillar attaches itself to a tree limb and remains motionless, looking to all the world like a dry, dead twig.

43. What backyard insect has the longest life span?

You probably won't find termites in your backyard, but if you live in a house made of wood, you may have these insects gnawing away at your floors and walls. Termites are among the world's most long-lived insects, with some reaching the ripe old age of forty years!

44. How do ticks find their victims?

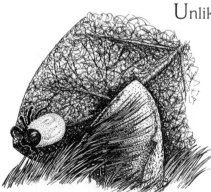

Unlike that other famous bloodsucker, the flea, ticks cannot jump. They can't fly either, so making their way to a dog, cat, or other host is a long and arduous process. Starting at ground level, the tick crawls slowly up the stem of a plant and out to the tip of a leaf. Stretching out its front legs, the tick waits, sometimes weeks or months, for an animal to pass by. When the victim brushes against the tick's leaf, the insect quickly grabs hold and rides away. After feeding on the host's blood, the tick drops to the ground and begins the process all over again.

If it chooses the wrong plant and no animal comes close enough, an unlucky tick may starve to death.

45. Why don't spiders get stuck in their own webs?

A common sight in just about any backyard is a large, circular spiderweb suspended between two plants or stretched across a path. Usually, a fat garden spider sits motionless at the center of the web, waiting for an insect to become entangled in the sticky strands. When this happens, the insect's struggles cause the web to vibrate, signaling to the spider that prey has been captured. Running over to it, the spider wraps the insect in silk and either consumes it on the spot or saves it for later.

Why don't spiders get caught in their own sticky traps as they make their way to the victim? Since only the outer strands circling the web are sticky,

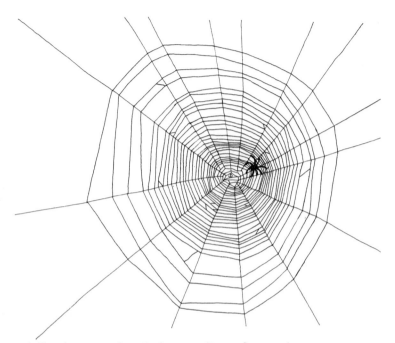

while the "spokes" that radiate from the center are dry, the spider is careful to walk only on the spokes when moving around the web. Even if she does accidentally step on a sticky strand, the spider is unlikely to get stuck, thanks to the thin film of oil covering her legs and feet.

46. How long does a spider's web last?

The main function of a spider's web is to ensnare flying insects, and after trapping a few struggling bugs, the web is usually ragged and full of holes. Rather than trying to repair it, the spider tears down the whole structure and builds a new one, a process that may take several hours. Many garden spiders spin an entirely new web every day.

47. How can you tell the temperature by listening to a cricket's song?

Open your window on a summer evening, and chances are you'll hear the distinctive chirping of crickets. One species that is found throughout the United States, the snowy tree cricket, produces a bell-like chirp that has a very unusual feature: The warmer the weather, the faster this cricket chirps. The relation-ship between the outside temperature and the snowy tree cricket's chirping rate is so precise that it is actu-ally possible to figure out the temperature by listen-ing to the cricket's song.

To do it, count the number of chirps you hear in thirteen seconds, add forty, and you'll have a pretty good estimate of the temperature in degrees Fahrenheit.

48. What are flying ants?

Although they spend most of their lives under-ground, there is one time when ants can fly: during the "marriage flight" that results in the formation of a new colony. It is usually toward the end of summer that an ant colony's queen begins to lay eggs that are somewhat unusual. Instead of developing into worker ants, the eggs hatch as winged males and fe-males whose only job is to reproduce.

No one knows exactly what sets them off, but on one warm, damp day, winged ants from all the colonies in the area leave their nests and soar into the sky. After mating in midair, both males and females fall back to earth.

As soon as she lands, the female rubs her body against the ground until her wings break off. Then she digs a burrow, seals herself off from the outside world, and begins to lay the eggs that will form a new colony. The new queen will remain sealed in the nest for the rest of her life, never seeing the light of day again.

For the male, the marriage flight is the last thing he will ever do—he dies as soon as mating is complete.

49. What backyard bug has the keenest vision in the insect kingdom?

Most scientists believe that the dragonfly has the best vision of any insect. The dragonfly's huge, compound eyes cover most of its head, meeting in a "seam" in the middle of its forehead. Each of the bulging eyes is made up of nearly 30,000 individual, six-sided facets. These facets detect light and movement and transmit this information to the dragonfly's brain to form a complete picture of its world. With its enormous eyes and its ability to swivel its head around on its slender neck, the dragonfly can see in almost all directions at once. This is bad news for anyone who tries to catch a dragonfly, and even worse news for the mosquitoes, gnats, and flies that are the dragonfly's favorite foods.

50. How did the ladybug get its name?

The ladybug, or lady-bird beetle, is one insect that people actu-ally like. The reason for the ladybug's popularity is its habit of eating aphids, mealybugs, and other plant-destroying pests. For years, farmers have successfully used ladybugs to protect their crops. In 1889, ladybugs saved the entire California citrus crop by devouring millions of scale insects that had infested the trees.

The ladybug got its name during the Middle Ages. In those days, people admired these tiny insects so much that they associated them with the Virgin Mary, calling them "the beetles of our Lady."

51. What's the difference between butterflies and moths?

Butterflies and moths both belong to the order Lepidoptera (which means "scaly winged"), and they are often very hard to tell apart. Here are some clues to help you figure out which is which:

❀ Butterflies are usually active during the daytime, whereas moths are mostly active at night.

❀ Butterflies are generally large and brightly colored, in contrast to moths, which are smaller and darker.

It is easy to find exceptions to these rules (day-flying moths and dull, drab butterflies), so to be absolutely sure, look at the insect's antennae. All butterflies have smooth antennae with a rounded knob at the end. The antennae of moths are either saw-toothed or covered with hairlike fringes or plumes.

52. Why are moths attracted to candle flames and other lights at night?

Flying toward (and sometimes into) bright lights at night is probably the habit for which moths are best known. In fact, the Navajo word for moth means "one that is fire crazy." The explanation for this strange behavior is something called "light compass orientation." Moths and some other night-flying insects find their way around by using the moon as a guide.

To fly in a straight line, the moth simply keeps

the moon in a certain position—off to the left, for example. If the position of the moon shifts to the center or the right, this tells the moth that it has flown off course. In response, the moth turns until the moon is on the left again.

This kind of navigation works only when the light, like that of the moon, is very far away. Unfortunately, moths don't know this, and they often try to use nearby electric lights or flames to navigate. Because the light is close to the moth, its position shifts as the moth flies past it. Trying to keep the light in the same position, the moth keeps turning toward it, eventually flying in circles around the flame.

53. What's the most amazing thing about fleas?

Fleas are not exactly "backyard" bugs, but if you have a pet dog or cat, you may well have had fleas in your house. Cat, dog, and human fleas all have tall, thin bodies that allow them to move easily through the forests of hair and fur in which they live. But the most amazing thing about fleas is their jumping ability. Even the tiniest flea can hop more than ten inches—the equivalent of a person making a leap of over 1,000 feet!

54. If my dog or cat has fleas, will they bite me too?

Unless your pet is very heavily infested with fleas, there is not much chance that you will even notice these insect pests. Surprisingly, you are most likely to be attacked *after* the flea-bitten dog or cat has been removed from the house.

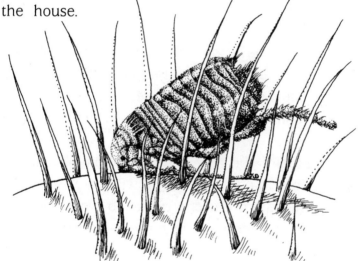

With their main food source gone, the hungry fleas left behind have no choice but to move on to people.

55. What are tent caterpillars?

If you have any cherry (or other fruit) trees in your backyard, you may have seen large, white tents hanging between the branches. Looking closely, you'll see that each silky structure contains hundreds of squirming, yellow-and-black caterpillars. As the morning sun warms them, the caterpillars leave the safety of their tent and crawl along the tree branches in search of leaves to eat. Away from the tent, they are in constant danger of being attacked by birds or ants. However, the tent caterpillar has a unique way of repelling these enemies. As it feeds, it extracts cyanide, a powerful poison, from the leaves of the cherry tree. If captured, the tent caterpillar spits out the cyanide liquid, which tastes so bad that the predator usually gives up and leaves the caterpillar alone.

Eventually, the tent caterpillar spins a cocoon and develops into a moth, which will mate and lay its eggs on the bark of the cherry tree to produce a new generation of caterpillars. In some years, there are so many tent caterpillars that they can strip a cherry orchard completely bare of its leaves.

56. How do termites eat wood?

There's not an animal in the world that can actually digest wood—so how do termites do it? The surprise is that termites can't do it either. They *eat* wood but then depend on tiny organisms called protozoa living in their stomachs to break down the wood particles and transform them into something the termite can digest. There are sometimes so many of these tiny creatures in a termite's stomach that they account for one-third of the insect's weight.

When termites are born they do not have these protozoa in their stomachs, so if they started eating wood right away they would starve to death. The very first thing a young termite eats is the waste products of an adult. In this way, it gets the important protozoa that will allow it to live on wood for the rest of its life.

57. Why do mosquitoes bite some people and leave others alone?

If you have ever been to camp or spent time outdoors on a summer evening, you have probably noticed that some people seem to get all the mosquito bites, while others get few or none. One reason for this difference is the amount of warmth that different people give off.

Mosquitoes use their tiny, heat-sensitive antennae to find and home in on their prey. Although the female's antennae are only about one-eighth of an inch long, she can detect a source of heat from several yards away. Once she has located a warm body, she flies toward it, picking up the scent of her victim as she draws near.

People who naturally give off a lot of heat, who are excited and active (which raises body temperature), or who wear dark clothing (which allows more heat to escape) are most likely to be attacked by mosquitoes. To keep from being a target, stay cool and calm and wear white or light-colored clothing.

58. How do insects breathe?

Unlike human beings, insects possess neither noses nor lungs, so it's obvious that they don't breathe in the same way we do. Insects get the oxygen they need through small holes that run in a line down each side of the body. Two of these openings, called spiracles, are usually found on each body segment.

To keep out dirt, dust, and water, each spiracle is equipped with a tiny trapdoor that remains closed most of the time. When the insect needs oxygen (for example, when it is flying or running), nerve impulses signal the trapdoors to open briefly and air flows into the insect's body.

59. Why are daddy longlegs spiders usually found in the basement?

With its long, slender legs and small body, the daddy longlegs is always in danger of drying out. To avoid this, it spends most of its time in cool or damp places such as bathrooms and cellars. Daddy long-legs spiders weave irregular webs of very fine silk and then hang upside down waiting for insects to pass by. They, along with other house spiders, are harmless to people. In fact, they help us out by eating mosquitoes, flies, and other insects we'd rather not have around. Compared to these buzzing nuisances, the shy and quiet daddy longlegs is the perfect houseguest.

60. What insect takes the longest time to develop into an adult?

The award in this category surely goes to the seventeen-year cicada, which spends a full seventeen years as a nymph (the stage between egg and adult). During this period, the cicada nymph lives underground, feeding on the sap of tree roots and growing very, very slowly. After seventeen years, the cicada crawls out of the soil, splits its skin, and makes the transformation into an adult.

Once it emerges, the adult cicada lives only about a month, just long enough to mate and (if it is a female) lay its eggs.

Some areas in Tennessee are home to two types of cicada: the northern seventeen-year cicada and

the southern thirteen-year cicada. Every 221 years, their cycles, coincide, and the two species hatch at the same time. During the next cicada plague (expected in the year 2089), parts of Tennessee will be overrun by hundreds of millions of cicadas per square mile.

61. What are beach fleas?

If you go to the beach, especially on a rough or stormy day, you may notice thousands of tiny animals hopping around frantically each time a wave breaks onto the shore. These little crustaceans, known as beach fleas or sandhoppers, live in a narrow strip of damp sand just a few feet up from the water. To survive, the beach flea needs to stay where the sand is damp. If it moves too far inland, the flea will die in the hot, dry sand, and it if ends up in the water, it may drown.

On stormy days, beach fleas spend all their time just trying to stay in their preferred habitat. When a receding wave sweeps them out to sea, the fleas turn and swim furiously toward land. Fleas that are tossed far up onto the beach by a breaking wave immediately begin hopping back toward the water in a desperate attempt to reach wetter sand. These swarms of fleas hopping seaward are a familiar sight at nearly every ocean beach.

62. Do centipedes really have 100 legs?

The house centipede (the kind you're most likely to see as it scurries under your refrigerator) can have as few as 30 legs or, for really big specimens, more than 350. All these legs enable house centipedes to move

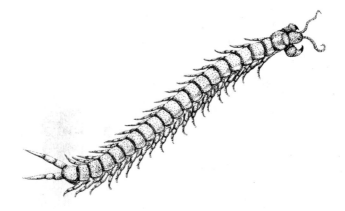

with incredible speed: One swift centipede was clocked at an incredible seventeen inches per second!

Although most people don't like to share their home with centipedes, they can actually be quite helpful. They are not dangerous to people, and they eat flies, cockroaches, and other common pests.

Losing a few legs is an occupational hazard for centipedes, but it's certainly not a tragedy. This insect can run perfectly well even if some of its legs are missing. Moreover, the next time the centipede molts, all its lost limbs will regenerate.

63. Are all wasps dangerous to humans?

The common wasps and yellow jackets with which most people are familiar do have a powerful sting that is always painful and sometimes dangerous. But most wasps pose no threat to humans, and some are even helpful, especially to farmers and gardeners.

The ichneumon wasp is a para-site that lives at the expense of other insect species, many of which are plant-destroying pests. That explains the ichneumon's popularity with people.

Each species of ichneumon wasp (there are 60,000 in all) specializes in a particular insect prey. One type attacks the larvae of the wood-eating horntail. Flitting from tree to tree, the wasp searches until it finds one containing horntail larvae. When it finds one, the wasp uses its long egg-laying tube (called an ovipositor) to drill a tiny hole in the tree and lay an egg into the body of the horntail. After hatching, the wasp larva begins to eat the horntail, killing it and minimizing further damage to the tree.

Drilling into tree trunks is difficult work, for which the wasp needs specialized equipment. In some ichneumon wasps, the ovipositor is nearly twice as long as the wasp's body. When drilling, the wasp arches the long ovipositor up and over its back and bores straight down into the tree.

64. What's the best way to spot an ichneumon wasp?

It isn't easy to spot this shy and secretive wasp, but if you're lucky enough to do so, you may be able to watch as it drills with its long ovipositor and lays its eggs. Ichneumon wasps are thin and delicate, with long antennae that they use to detect their prey. It is thought that the wasp uses its antennae to feel for the faint vibrations of the horntail larvae feeding deep within the tree.

The wasp pictured is one of the largest of the ichneumons. Its body measures two to three inches long, and the threadlike ovipositor adds another two to four inches. The best place to see these wasps is along the borders of wooded areas, as they move from tree to tree feeling with their antennae for prey. Another way is to check your window screens at

night. Several ichneumon species are attracted to light and will make their way into your house if they can.

65. What's the best time of year to see a praying mantis?

The praying mantis is one of the most spectacular insects you're likely to encounter in your backyard. Bright green and nearly four inches long, the mantis has powerful front legs that it uses to snap up its insect prey.

Mantis nymphs hatch in late spring and continue to grow for the next few months. Late summer is the ideal time to spot a gigantic praying mantis perched among the plants in your garden as it waits for an unsuspecting insect to come along. Because of its green color and its habit of remaining motionless, the mantis blends in well with its surroundings. So despite its large size, it is easy to overlook.

You may have more success finding praying mantis egg cases during fall and winter. These cases, which look like globs of hardened foam, are usually attached to the stems of weeds and grasses. The best place to look for them is in overgrown fields, along roadsides, or anywhere else that tall weeds grow.

66. What common insect has been around since the days of the dinosaurs?

About 350 million years ago, when dinosaurs roamed the earth, the first cockroaches appeared. But unlike dinosaurs, cockroaches are still with us, and they are doing better than ever.

One reason for their success is their adaptability. Cockroaches can live in nearly any environment (although they prefer the tropics), and they will eat almost anything, including human food, bookbindings, fingernail clippings, and even other cockroaches.

They also possess amazing reproductive powers. During their lifetime, which may be as long as a year or more, a pair of roaches can produce up to 400,000 eggs.

Getting rid of cockroaches can be very difficult. Because they eat such a wide variety of things, it is almost impossible to eliminate all their food sources. And the average roach can live for several weeks without food, anyway. They can't go quite as long without water, and this explains why people almost never see cockroaches in their cars. Even in the most crumb-filled cars, there is rarely anything to drink, so cockroaches stay away.

67. How many eyes do spiders have?

The answer to this question isn't as easy as it seems, because different kinds of spiders have different numbers of eyes. Eight eyes are the most common, but some spiders have six, four, one, or even no eyes at all! Most spiders, even those with eight eyes, do

not see very well. Instead, they rely on thousands of tiny hairs covering their legs and body to give them information about touch and taste.

The spider with the best vision is the jumping spider, which stalks and pounces on its prey in much the same way as a cat stalks a mouse. Strangely enough, different eyes do different jobs as this spider hunts.

When an insect comes within twelve to fifteen inches of the jumping spider, it is detected by a row of "secondary" eyes that specialize in sensing *movement*. At this point, the spider cannot tell what the prey animal is, just that there's something moving out there.

When the insect comes closer than eight inches, the spider turns to face it and the main eyes take over. These eyes specialize in seeing *details*, and as they focus on the approaching object, the spider decides whether it is truly something to eat. If it is, the jumping spider stalks, pounces, and finally devours its unlucky victim.

3

Moles, Mice, & Other Mammals

68. Why do white-tailed deer have white tails?

White-tailed deer are a very common sight in rural (and some suburban) areas throughout the United States. The farther away you live from a city, the greater your chances of seeing one or more white-tailed deer nibbling on plants in your backyard. The bright white fur that gives this deer its name can be seen underneath the tail and on the animal's rump. When the deer is resting or grazing, it keeps its tail down, so that the white area is not visible. But when danger threatens, the deer lifts its tail, exposing the white patch, and bounds away. By revealing its tail patch, the fleeing deer sends a warning signal to other deer that danger is near. When they see the white flash, all the deer nearby turn and run after the leader. Knowing about this signal can be helpful if you are try-ing to watch deer in the woods. Don't wear white or other light-colored clothing, which the deer may see as a sign of danger. Tan, brown, or other dark colors will allow you to get closer to the animals without scaring them away.

69. Why do raccoons wash their food?

The raccoon's habit of dunking its food in water be-fore eating is so well known that it earned this animal its scientific name, *Procyon lotor* (*lotor* means "washer"). Surprisingly, though, this behavior has only been observed in raccoons living in captivity (in zoos or as pets). Raccoons in the wild have never been seen washing their food.

For years, scientists were puzzled by this difference. They finally concluded that captive raccoons are not really *washing* their food when they dip it in the water. Instead, they are going through the motions of *finding* food in their water dish.

Wild raccoons often catch frogs, turtles, and other food in ponds or streams by dabbling in the shallow water with their front paws. A captive raccoon sees its water dish as a miniature pond and expects to find food there. When the dish contains only water, the frustrated raccoon compensates by dropping its food in the water dish and then "finding" it by dabbling in the water with its paws. It is this food-finding behavior that looks so much like washing.

70. What happens to animals when they hibernate?

To survive the winter cold, some backyard animals (especially birds) migrate to warmer climates. Others go into a long winter sleep called hibernation. When an animal hibernates, its body processes slow down. Body temperature and heartbeat drop, and breathing slows to a fraction of its normal rate. Sometimes the change is quite dramatic. The thirteen-lined ground squirrel, which lives throughout the central United States and Canada, normally breathes between 100 and 200 times a minute. When it is hibernating, this squirrel breathes only once or twice a minute, and its heart beats only about five times a minute. Though it appears to be sleeping deeply, the squirrel will wake up almost immediately if it is disturbed.

71. Where do squirrels build their nests?

Although they can often be spotted scampering along the ground, squirrels spend most of their time in trees. They usually don't venture far from their "home" tree, so if you see squirrels in a particular tree, there's a good chance they have made a nest there as well.

A cavity in the trunk of an old tree makes an ideal nest. Gray squirrels sometimes use holes originally pecked out by woodpeckers, gnawing away at the opening until it is large enough for the animals to enter.

In warm weather, squirrels sometimes build nests among the branches of a tree, and these are much easier to see than cavity nests. The best place to look for these "outdoor" nests is about forty feet above the ground, in a tree fork close to the trunk. The nest itself looks like a ball of leaves and is usually a little more than one foot across. If you watch for a while, you may be lucky enough to see the squirrels and their babies poking their heads out of the hollow leaf nest.

72. Why do squirrels have such big tails?

One of the most impressive tails in the animal kingdom is that of the common backyard squirrel. This long, bushy tail can be almost as big as the squirrel itself.

A very important function of a squirrel's tail is to

help the animal keep its balance as it runs along branches or does a high-wire act on power lines. (Think of a tightrope walker holding a long pole for balance and you'll understand the usefulness of the squirrel's long tail.)

Squirrels also use their tails to communicate with each other. Tail flicking is a clue that the squirrel is alarmed, while a fluffed-up tail signals that it is feeling aggressive. Squirrels also wave and "shiver" their tails when approaching the opposite sex during the breeding season.

One of the most practical ways a squirrel uses its tail is to keep warm in the winter and cool in the summer. When the temperature drops, the squirrel curls up in its nest with its tail wrapped around its body like a blanket. In hot weather, the squirrel uses its tail as a sunshade to protect itself from the sun's burning rays.

73. How long do squirrels live?

In captivity, gray squirrels have been known to live as long as twenty years. In the wild, however, squirrels face danger every day. Falls from trees, car accidents, and encounters with owls, neighborhood dogs, and other predators take their toll, and most squirrels do not live past age ten.

74. Do flying squirrels really fly?

Very few people have ever seen a flying squirrel. But it's not because they are rare—flying squirrels are found throughout much of the eastern and western

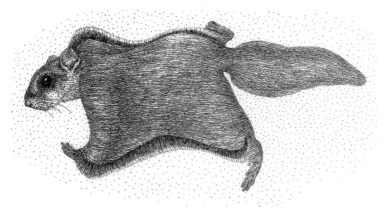

United States, and some may be living right in your neighborhood. The reason you probably haven't seen them is that, unlike the common gray squirrel, flying squirrels are active only at night.

The flying squirrel does not actually fly. Instead, it uses a loose fold of skin that stretches from the front to back legs as a parachute to glide incredible distances. When these skin flaps are extended, the flying squirrel looks almost like a kite. Starting from a head-down position on a tree trunk, the flying squirrel spreads its flaps and takes off. It can sometimes glide hundreds of feet before coming down to earth.

75. How can I tell if I have moles in my backyard?

Moles are small, furry animals that live virtually all of their lives underground. Because they rarely come to the surface, it's not easy to spot a mole. You'll know you have them if you see evidence of their subterranean tunnels: small piles of dirt (called molehills) or long ridges of earth that the moles push up as they excavate just beneath the surface.

Most gardeners don't like moles because of the damage they do as they tunnel under lawns and gardens. But these little animals can be beneficial. They eat many insect pests, and their tunnels actually help loosen and cultivate the soil. Using its powerful claws, a mole can tunnel up to fifteen feet an hour.

76. What's the weirdest mole?

Of the six species of mole in North America, the strangest is certainly the star-nosed mole. With no external ears and very tiny eyes, this mole is nearly

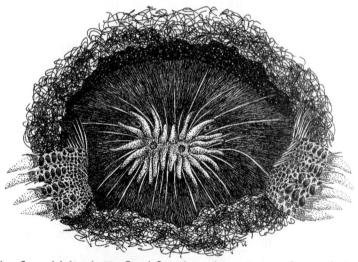

deaf and blind. To find food and navigate through its underground tunnels, the star-nosed mole relies on an octopuslike ring of pink tentacles surrounding its nose. As it creeps through a tunnel, the mole feels its way with these sensitive tentacles, much like a person using outstretched arms to make his way carefully through a darkened room.

Besides guiding the mole in its travels underground, the tentacles help keep dirt out of the mole's nose as it excavates new tunnels. The star-nosed mole is also an excellent swimmer and has even been known to plug its nostrils with its tentacles while swimming to keep the water out.

77. Why are skunks black and white?

Think about some familiar backyard animals, such as squirrels, chipmunks, and raccoons. With their dull brown or gray coats, these animals blend in easily with their surroundings, which helps them hide from potential enemies.

The skunk, however, has no need to avoid its enemies. Using a pair of scent glands under its tail, this little animal can defend itself against almost any predator by spraying it with a horrible-smelling liquid musk. In most cases, however, a confrontation never reaches the spraying stage. Just one look at the skunk's bright black-and-white pattern is warning enough, and most animals (including humans) turn and run at the first sight of a skunk. Because they scare enemies away so easily, skunks actually use their scent much less often than people imagine.

There is one predator that isn't deterred by the skunk's scent. The great horned owl has a very poor sense of smell, and it also has a special membrane that slides across its eyes, protecting them from the burning liquid musk. Because great horned owls are immune to its weapons, they are among the skunk's worst enemies.

78. Are bats really blind?

Contrary to what most people believe, the phrase "blind as a bat" is absolutely false. Bats can see, but like many nocturnal (night active) animals, they rely on other senses much more than they rely on vision.

The bat's most amazing characteristic is its ability to navigate and hunt at night by listening to high-frequency sound pulses that it produces. These sounds, too high-pitched for humans to hear, are made through the bat's nose or mouth and are sometimes amplified by grotesque, leaflike structures on the nose. The bat then uses its ultrasensitive ears to pick up the echoes of the sounds bouncing off objects in the environment. By focusing on the time it takes for echoes to come back, the bat knows how far away things are. Even very tiny objects can be detected by *echolocation,* as this process is called, and it is the way bats find moths and other insect prey.

Most backyard bats are insect eaters, and one bat can consume hundreds of moths, mosquitoes, and other flying bugs in the course of an evening.

79. Why are rabbits sometimes called cottontails?

North America's most common rabbit, the eastern cottontail, gets its name from its short, fluffy tail. On top, the tail is the same grayish brown as the rest of the rabbit, but underneath, the color is a pure cottony white.

Like the white-tailed deer, the cottontail rabbit flashes its white tail to warn other rabbits of danger. The cottontail's large eyes and sensitive ears enable

it to stay on guard at all times, so if you have rabbits in your yard, the most you may see of them is a quick white tail flash as they bolt for cover. The best time to spot cottontails is when they are foraging for food at twilight or just before sunrise.

80. Why are fawns (young deer) speckled brown and white while adult deer are all brown?

The young of many animals, including deer, have coat colors or patterns that look very different from those of their parents. Even the most brilliant tropical birds often have chicks whose feathers are drab and dull. This difference occurs because young animals are sometimes unable to escape danger by running or flying away, so they do the next best thing: They hide. Drab fur or feathers camouflage the young animal, helping it to blend into its surroundings, so a predator is less likely to notice it.

In the case of the deer, it seems strange that a brown-and-white-spotted coat should provide more camouflage than an all brown one. But in the deer's woodland habitat, the white-speckled fur blends in with the dappled sunlight, making a motionless fawn almost impossible to see.

Adult deer are very swift runners and can usually escape danger by darting away. As the fawn gets older and faster, the protective brown-and-white coloration becomes less important for survival, and the fawn's coat color changes to pure brown.

81. Why do squirrels and chipmunks hoard nuts?

Both squirrels and chipmunks are well known for stuffing their cheeks with nuts and seeds and then burying these treasures to dig up later. The chipmunk, whose roomy cheek pouches may extend as far as its shoulders, is so famous for this behavior that its scientific name means "hoarder."

Although squirrels and chipmunks do sometimes dig up stored seeds when food is scarce, they just as often abandon them completely. Some of these forgotten seeds eventually take root and sprout into new trees. In some forests, squirrels unwittingly play a major role as tree planters.

82. I thought rats came out only at night, but sometimes in the park I see them running around in broad daylight. What's going on?

It's true that rats are basically nocturnal, foraging for food at night and curling up in their burrows during the day. When you see a rat in the daytime, a likely explanation is that it didn't get enough to eat the night before.

Rats live in small family groups headed by one or two large males. These dominant rats are the first to eat, and they usually eat the most. If food is scarce, they may not share it with lower-ranking members of the group. When this happens, the low-ranking rats are forced to wait until daylight, when the bigger rats are sleeping off their dinners, to go out and search for something to eat.

83. How does a beaver gnaw down trees without getting wood chips in its mouth?

Beavers are rodents, and like all other members of this group (including gophers, woodchucks, rats, mice, and squirrels), they have large front teeth, specialized for gnawing. These teeth are a rodent's most valuable tool. Beavers rely on their powerful front teeth to cut down trees, gophers use them to excavate tunnels in the earth, and squirrels use them to crack nuts. To do all these things without getting a mouthful of wood chips, dirt, or nutshells, a rodent has a specially designed mouth. In between the front teeth and the back teeth is a wide gap with no teeth at all. When it wants to gnaw, the animal pulls its lips sideways into the gap, much like when you suck your cheeks in to make a "fish face." This closes off its mouth while the front teeth remain exposed. By doing this, a rodent can chisel away at wood and dirt without getting an unexpected mouthful.

84. Why do rats, mice, and rabbits constantly gnaw on things?

One of the worst things about having mice or rats in your house, or rabbits in your garden, is the damage they can do with their teeth. Rodents quickly chew through cardboard, wood, and even metal to get to food, and a single rabbit can eat an entire vegetable garden in no time. In all these cases, the animal's urge to chew is more than just a desire for food. The teeth of rodents and rabbits grow constantly and quickly—up to five inches a year for rats and rabbits. If they did not gnaw regularly, these animals would be in trouble, for their teeth would eventually grow so long that they would not be able to chew or even open their mouths. Unable to eat, they would soon starve to death.

Gnawing also sharpens the teeth, creating a chisel-like edge that helps rats, mice, and squirrels chew their way into your house.

85. How can you tell a rabbit from a hare?

Everyone has heard of Beatrix Potter's Peter Rabbit and the March Hare from *Alice in Wonderland,* but what's the difference? It is not always easy to tell, and their names sometimes just add to the confusion. For instance, a jackrabbit is really a hare, while a Belgian hare is actually a rabbit.

In general, hares are bigger than rabbits and have longer legs and ears. But the best way to tell one from the other is to look at the babies. Young rabbits (called kits) are blind and completely helpless at birth, whereas young hares (called leverets) begin to hop around after just a few hours.

Like Peter, the cottontails you may see in your garden are rabbits. But don't expect to check it out for yourself—these shy and secretive bunnies hide their nests so well that you will probably never see a newborn.

4

Cold-Blooded Creatures & Other Weird Wildlife

86. Are there snakes in my backyard?

For most people, the sight of a snake crawling around the yard would come as quite a shock. But just because you have never seen one in your neighborhood, don't assume that snakes don't live there. Several kinds, including garter snakes, corn snakes, brown snakes, and rat snakes, can be found in vacant lots, wooded areas, abandoned buildings, and almost anywhere else that food is plentiful. (Depending on the snake, favorite foods can include earthworms, frogs, mice, and even baby birds.)

The main reason snakes are hard to spot is their secretive nature. At the slightest disturbance, they tend to slither quietly away. In the northern parts of the United States, snakes are only active during warm weather, spending the fall, winter, and early spring hibernating in caves or burrows.

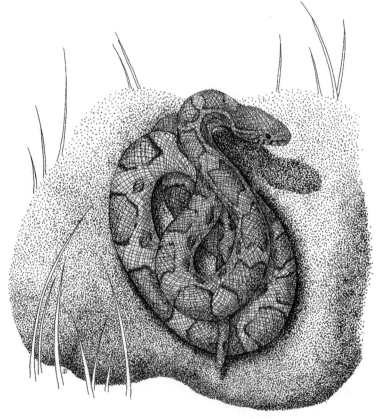

On warm days, snakes may come out to bask in the sun. When it gets too hot, though, they retreat to cool, dark spots.

The best way to find out if you have snakes living near you is to watch for the papery dry skin that the snake leaves behind each time it sheds.

87. How did the milk snake get its name?

If you live on or near a farm, you have probably seen, or at least heard about, the milk snake. This medium-sized, reddish brown snake often lives around barns and other farm buildings. Because of this, legend has it that milk snakes drink milk directly from the cows' udders. This story is undoubtedly false—what cow would stand still for a snake with a mouthful of razor-sharp teeth? Most likely, milk snakes live near barns because of the plentiful supply of their favorite food: mice, rats, and other small animals.

88. How do rattlesnakes get their rattles?

Depending on where you live, you may have rattlesnakes living closer to your backyard than you would like. Rattlesnakes are among this country's most feared reptiles, and anyone who hears this snake's distinctive warning rattle will never forget the sound.

When a rattlesnake is born, it has no rattle, just a tiny, hard button on the end of its tail. The rattle begins to grow when the snake sheds its skin for the first time (leaving it behind like an inside-out sock). All that remains of the old skin is a hardened ring, which takes its place in front of the button at the end of the tail. Each time the snake sheds, another ring is added to the rattle.

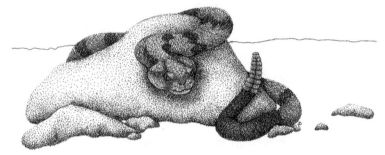

Like most other snakes, rattlesnakes vibrate their tails when they feel threatened or alarmed. You would never notice this behavior in snakes without rattles, but when the rattlesnake shakes its tail, the loose-fitting rings of skin rattle against each other, producing this snake's signature sound.

89. Is it true that you can tell a rattlesnake's age by the size of its rattle?

Up to a point. A baby snake that has not yet shed its skin has no rattle at all, just a button at the end of its tail. After that, rattlesnakes shed three to five times a year, so if you see a snake with a six-ring rattle, you'll know the snake is just over a year old.

You would expect that as a rattlesnake gets older, its rattle would get bigger and bigger. But the longer the rattle gets, the more fragile it becomes, and eventually the end of it (along with the button) breaks off as the snake crawls over rocks, logs, and other hazards in its path. So very old rattlesnakes usually have shorter and more worn-looking rattles than snakes that are just a few years old.

90. Why do frogs croak?

One of the main reasons that frogs croak is to find a mate. If you're near a pond on a summer evening, you may well hear the almost deafening chorus of male frogs as they try to attract females.

Males usually arrive first at the breeding area, so their loud calls help the voiceless females to home in on the right spot. Once the females arrive, the croak serves a slightly different purpose. Frogs breed at night, and in the dark a male frog will grab anything within reach. If he wraps his legs around something that croaks back, the amorous amphibian knows he has accidentally grabbed a male, and he quickly lets go. He keeps trying until he finds a partner who doesn't respond with a croak— only then

i s he as- s u r e d o f h a v i n g found a female.

91. How far can a frog jump?

With their powerful hind legs, frogs are well known for their jumping abilities. The bullfrog can hop nearly nine times its own length for a spectacular leap of six feet. The leopard frog, which measures only about five inches long, can jump over five feet— or about thirteen times its body length. With this feat, the leopard frog holds the title of best long jumper in North America.

92. How is a toad like a snake?

Although they are different in many respects, toads and snakes are alike in one way: They both shed their skins when they become too small. In snakes, shedding is a major project, which can take several hours. Toads, on the other hand, shed their skins so quickly that most people aren't even aware that they do it.

 After the toad has been feeding steadily for a

while, its skin becomes too tight and soon splits down the back. Rubbing furiously with its hands, the toad peels off the old skin. Unlike the snake, which leaves its shed skin behind, the toad rolls its cast-off skin into a ball and swallows it.

It takes only a few minutes for a toad to shed its skin, and the whole process may occur as often as every three days.

93. How does a rattlesnake find its prey?

Vision, smell, and hearing are some of the more common senses that animals use to locate their prey. But rattlesnakes find food in quite a different way: by sensing the warmth of the animal's body!

All rattlesnakes are equipped with a pair of heat-detecting pits between the eye and the nostril. The pits are incredibly sensitive to warmth and can register a temperature change of as little as .002 degrees.

To capture prey, whether by day or night, the rattlesnake rests quietly, waiting for the rise in temperature that indicates a warm-blooded animal nearby. Even a tiny mouse passing six inches in front of the snake's nose is enough to trigger the heat-sensitive pits. As soon as the rattlesnake gets the signal, it lunges forward and strikes at its unsuspecting prey.

94. Why do frogs and toads blink?

Like humans and most other animals, frogs and toads blink frequently to keep their eyeballs moist and to sweep dirt and other debris out of the eyes. But frogs and toads have another, more unusual, reason for blinking: It helps them swallow their food!

In people, the bony skull surrounds and protects the eyeballs. But the eyes of frogs and toads are not fixed in position, so when these amphibians blink, the bulging eyes are pushed down into the roof of the mouth. This comes in handy when a frog or toad catches a fly or earthworm. As it blinks repeatedly, the frog or toad squeezes its eyes down toward its mouth, helping to push the food down its throat.

95. How do earthworms tunnel through the ground?

Amazing as it seems, the soft little earthworm can make its way through even the most rock-hard dirt.

It does this by literally eating everything in its path, including pieces of soil, decaying leaves, and other debris. Anything edible is digested, providing food for the worm, while the undigested matter passes through its body.

96. Why do birds have such a hard time pulling worms out of the ground?

One of the most familiar sights of spring is a red-breasted robin on the front lawn, tugging on a fat earthworm. As every robin knows, it is no easy job to dislodge a worm from its underground burrow. Although an earthworm looks smooth and slimy, its body is actually covered with tiny bristles. The worm uses special muscles to extend the bristles or pull them back into its body. When it wants to move around, the worm retracts the bristles into tiny sacs in the body wall. To stay put, the worm anchors itself in the ground by pushing the bristles into the dirt walls of the burrow.

97. Can earthworms see?

Look closely at the next earthworm you meet, and you'll find that it has no eyes. But although earthworms cannot see in the same way people can, they are very sensitive to light. In fact, earthworms have receptors all over their bodies that respond to changes in brightness.

So when a hungry bird ap-

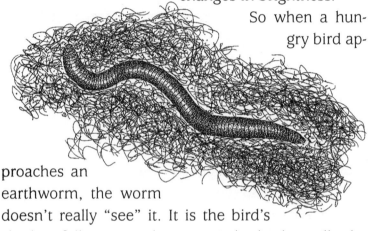

proaches an earthworm, the worm doesn't really "see" it. It is the bird's shadow falling over the worm's body that tells the worm it is time to retreat into its burrow.

98. Why do so many earthworms come out on the sidewalk when it rains?

Most people assume that earthworms come to the surface during heavy rains to avoid drowning in the water that floods their tunnels. In fact, worms can live totally submerged in water, so drowning isn't the problem. But the rainwater that filters down through the ground contains very little oxygen, so the real reason earthworms come to the surface is to breathe.

Once above ground, earthworms are very sensitive to light, and even a brief exposure to the sun's rays can paralyze them. Unable to crawl back into their burrows, they eventually dry out and die on the sidewalk.

99. Why do slugs and snails leave a slimy trail wherever they go?

Have you ever tried to go down a slide in a wet bathing suit? If so, you probably found that a damp suit on a dry slide made for a slow and unsatisfying ride down. This is exactly the situation a moist slug

faces as it tries to inch across the dry earth. To solve the problem, snails and slugs secrete a slimy mucus that lets them glide across the ground with ease. The slippery mucus also protects the slug's soft body from rocks, sticks, and other sharp objects in its path. Slugs have even been known to slither safely over razor blades, with only their mucus for protection!

100. Does a snail ever outgrow its shell?

Have you ever wondered what would happen if a garden snail got too big for the home it carries on its back? Fortunately, that is never a problem because as the snail grows the shell grows along with it.

Snails build their own shells, starting at the very center of the spiral. The shell is produced by a fold of skin called the mantle, which secretes the shell material. Throughout the snail's lifetime, the mantle continues to produce secretions. As this happens, more and more "turns" are added to the spiral shell, creating an ever-larger home for the growing snail.

When the snail dies, its home does not go to waste. The most frequent new tenant is a hermit crab, which you may see scuttling along the beach in a cast-off snail shell.

101. What are barnacles?

If you've ever visited a city waterfront with its docks and piers, you have probably noticed hundreds of cone-shaped barnacles clinging to wooden pilings at low tide. Many people don't realize that barnacles are animals, related to such well-known crustaceans as crabs and shrimp.

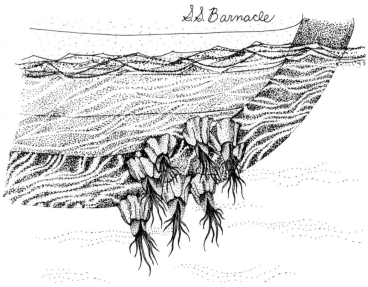

S.S. Barnacle

Although they spend their adult lives glued to one spot, young barnacles swim freely through the water, looking for a place to settle down. When they find the perfect spot—the bottom of a boat, a rock, or a pier—a strange transformation occurs.

First, the young barnacle glues itself head downward to its chosen spot. Then it begins to grow hard plates that eventually surround and protect the barnacle's soft body. Finally, the legs change into delicate, fringed fans called cirri.

When the tide comes in and the barnacle is underwater, it opens a small trapdoor and extends its cirri, which comb the water for bits of food. At low tide, the barnacle is left high and dry. To survive until the next high tide, the little barnacle pulls in its legs, snaps its trapdoor shut, and waits until the water rises again.

Appendix

Here are a few organizations that can give you more information about wildlife and nature.

National Audubon Society
P.O. Box 52529
Boulder, Colorado 80322

Sierra Club
85 Second Street
San Francisco, California 94105

Wildlife Conservation Society
Bronx Zoo
Bronx, New York 10460

Further Reading

You can find books about all kinds of backyard wildlife on the shelves of your local library. Here are a few suggestions to get you started.

BIRDS

Bash, Barbara. *Urban Roosts: Where Birds Nest in the City*. San Francisco: Sierra Club Books, 1990.

Lerner, Carol. *Backyard Birds of Winter*. New York: Morrow Junior Books, 1994.

Snedden, Robert. *What Is a Bird?* San Francisco: Sierra Club Books, 1993.

INSECTS

Barker, Will. *Familiar Insects of America*. New York: Harper & Row, 1960.

Snedden, Robert. *What Is an Insect?* San Francisco: Sierra Club Books, 1993.

Further Reading

AMPHIBIANS

Parker, Steve. *Frogs and Toads*. San Francisco: Sierra Club Books, 1994.

MAMMALS

Bailey, John. *Our Wild Animals*. New York: Thomas Nelson & Sons, 1965.

WATCHING WILDLIFE

Arnosky, Jim. *Crinkleroot's Book of Animal Tracking*. New York: Bradbury Press, 1969.

Arnosky, Jim. *Secrets of a Wildlife Watcher*. New York: Lothrop, Lee & Shepard Books, 1983.

Rowland–Entwistle, Theodore. *Animal Homes*. New York: Warwick Press, 1978.

Index